Breaking Free

Making Liberty in Christ a Reality in Life

Leader Guide

Beth Moore
and Dale McCleskey

LifeWay Press
Nashville, Tennessee

ISBN 0-7673-9113-6

Dewey Decimal Classification: 248.843
Subject Heading: WOMEN-RELIGIOUS LIFE \ BIBLE.O.T. ISAIAH-
STUDY AND TEACHING

Scripture quotations identified NIV are from the Holy Bible,
New International Version
Copyright © 1973, 1978, 1984
by International Bible Society

Order additional copies of this book by writing to Customer Service Center, MSN 113;
127 Ninth Avenue, North; Nashville, TN 37234-0113; by calling toll free 1 (800) 458-2772;
by faxing 1 (615) 251-5933; by ordering online at *www.lifeway.com;* by emailing
customerservice@lifeway.com; or by visiting a LifeWay Christian Store.

For information about adult discipleship and family resources, training, and events,
visit our Web site at *www.lifeway.com/discipleplus.*

Dale McCleskey, Editor
Paula Savage, Art Director
Linda Coombs, Assistant Editor
Rhonda Porter Delph, Manuscript Assistant
Chris Adams, Women's Enrichment Ministry Specialist

Printed in the United States of America

LifeWay Press
127 Ninth Avenue, North
Nashville, Tennessee 37234-0151

*As God works through us, we will help people and churches know Jesus Christ and seek His kingdom
by providing biblical solutions that spiritually transform individuals and churches.*

Introduction

Breaking Free by Beth Moore is an in-depth study based on the Book of Isaiah. The goal of our study is to make liberty in Christ a reality in life. From the Book of Isaiah, members will identify five primary benefits of the Christian life. They will then explore what keeps believers from living in a daily experience of those benefits and how to develop a lifestyle of obedience.

This guide has been prepared to equip you to plan and lead a study of *Breaking Free* for groups in your church or community. You will find administrative guidance, help for planning and promoting the study, and step-by-step instructions for conducting 11 group-study sessions. To prepare adequately, you also need to watch the leadership segment on tape 1 of the videotape series provided in the leader kit. In it author Beth Moore and Chris Adams, Women's Enrichment Ministry Specialist at LifeWay Christian Resources, discuss additional administrative suggestions for offering this study.

COURSE OVERVIEW

This in-depth course was designed to be completed over 11 weeks through a combination of daily, individual study and weekly group sessions.

Individual study. Each participant needs a copy of the *Breaking Free* member book, which contains reading assignments and activities designed to reinforce and apply learning. The member book is divided into an introduction and 10 weeks of content. Every week's material contains 5 daily lessons, each requiring about 45 minutes to complete. Participants complete the daily reading and the learning activities at home in preparation for the weekly group sessions.

Group sessions. Participants meet once each week for a two-hour group session that guides them to discuss and apply what they have learned during their daily, individual study. The small-group portion of this session encourages accountability and allows members to benefit from the insights of other participants as they process the material they have studied during the week. The small groups also help build relationships as participants share prayer concerns and pray together. In the large-group time, members watch weekly video presentations in which Beth Moore enhances the material in the book and concludes each session with additional truths and challenges.

GROUP-SESSION FORMAT

For members to receive the greatest possible benefit from this study, plan for a 2-hour group session each week, plus a 15-minute check-in period. Following this format ensures that members receive the blessings of intimate experiences with God through daily study, support and fellowship through small-group discussions, and inspiration through the video presentations. The session-leadership suggestions in this guide reflect the following schedule, although times shown here are arbitrary selections.

8:45   Child care open, attendance and homework check (15 mins.)

9:00   Large group—welcome, worship, and prayer (15 mins.)

9:15   Small groups (45 mins.)
- Prayer (5 mins.)
- Discussion of principal questions (20 mins.)
- Discussion of personal discussion questions (20 mins.)

10:00   Break and return to large group (5 mins.)

10:05   Large group (55 mins.)
- Video presentation (50 mins.)
- Closing assignment and prayer (5 mins.)

11:00   Dismiss

This schedule is ideal for a weekday or a weeknight study. It may also be followed for the church's Discipleship Training period if the study is begun an hour early and does not interfere with other church activities.

Some elements of this format may be adjusted to your preferences or needs. For example, you may prefer to add time for a longer break between the small- and large-group periods. Feel free to adjust the schedule, but we encourage you not to omit any one of the three key ingredients of this learning model:

(1) individual study of the member book at home,
(2) small-group discussion of the principal questions and the personal discussion questions in each week's material in the member book, and
(3) large-group viewing of the videos.

Here is an overview of the procedures for each segment of the group session.

Child care open, attendance and homework check (15 mins.). Allow time for mothers to leave their children in child-care facilities before the session begins. Each participant needs to check in and have homework reviewed by the small-group facilitator outside the large-group meeting room before entering. The facilitator does not check for correct responses but simply verifies that each member's work was done.

Large group—welcome, worship, and prayer (15 mins.). The large-group leader is responsible for convening the group and conducting this portion of the session. You may wish to plan special music or select an appropriate hymn or praise song for the group to sing. End this segment with prayer for the day's learning experience.

Small-group discussion (45 mins.). If the number of participants is small, remain in one group for this segment. If you enroll more than 12 people, however, plan for a small group for every 10 to 12 people and enlist a small-group facilitator for each group. These facilitators are responsible for taking prayer requests, having a prayer time (5 mins.), and guiding participants to discuss the principal questions (20 mins.) and personal discussion questions (20 mins.) in each week's material in the member book.

Return to large group (5 mins.). This transitional time allows time for a brief break. Provide light refreshments if desired.

Video presentation (50 mins.). A video presentation by Beth Moore is provided in the leader kit for each week's group session. The large-group leader should play the appropriate video at this time. Participants complete the corresponding video response sheet at the end of each week's material in their member books as they view the video. Beth concludes each video segment with a personal word and an additional challenge.

Closing assignment and prayer (5 mins.). The large-group leader encourages participants to complete the next week's daily assignments and closes with a prayer of praise or thanksgiving.

OPTIONAL FORMAT

A format of an introductory session plus 2 hours per week for 10 weeks is ideal for *Breaking Free;* however, you may need another option to fit your group's situation. Many groups study these materials with an alternate schedule. The problem with studying on a schedule other than one unit per week is that members do not get into the regular habit of daily Bible study.

If you adopt an alternate plan, please take steps to encourage members to study the Bible daily. If your group can only meet for one hour per week, consider viewing the video one week and conducting the group study the next. To maintain the continuity of daily study, encourage members to complete the daily work in the member book during the first week. Then, encourage them to review the work daily during the second week. Ask them to write down their answers to the Principal Questions and Personal Discussion Questions each day during their review.

Some groups meet once a month. If your group meets on some schedule other than weekly or bi-weekly, consider using an aid to encourage daily Bible study. One such resource is called *Day By Day in God's Kingdom.* It is a discipleship journal built around six Christian disciplines. It allows disciples to record their spiritual journeys as they study courses such as *Breaking Free.* Ask your members to complete the work in *Breaking Free* during the first week of the month and to review the material the week before the group meets.

RESOURCES

These resources are available for leaders and participants.

- *Breaking Free* (member book) provides an introduction and 10 weeks of daily, biblical studies on making liberty in Christ a reality in life. The book also includes viewer guides for video segments. Each participant needs a copy of the member book. Order item 0-7673-9112-8.

- *Breaking Free Leader Kit* contains one copy of the member book; this leader guide; and six videotapes. Five of the videotapes feature 10 lectures in which Beth Moore teaches material related to the content of the book. A sixth video provides content for an introductory group session, administrative guidance for organizing and leading the study, and a brief promotion/enlistment segment that includes a 30-second spot for use on local television stations. These videos are provided in the leader kit and are not available separately. Order item 0-7673-3402-7.

- *Breaking Free Leader Guide* (the guide you are now reading) offers step-by-step directions for facilitating 11 group sessions, using *Breaking Free* and the videotapes included in the leader kit. This guide, one copy of which is included in the leader kit, is available separately. Order item number 0-7673-9113-6.

- *Breaking Free Audiotapes* include the audio portions of Beth Moore's video presentations on 6 cassette tapes, with a 16-page listening guide. Although the tapes were designed for individual study, a leader may wish to use them for personal review and inspiration. Order item 0-7673-9111-X.

You will also need the following materials.

- Registration tables
- Small signs that indicate divisions of the alphabet—A–E, F–J, K–O, P–S, T–Z, for example.
- Registration cards
- An attendance sheet for each small-group facilitator
- Name tags
- Pencils
- Bibles
- A videotape player and monitor

CHOOSING LEADERS

The following are descriptions of the roles and responsibilities of leaders.

Large-group leader. This leader is not a teacher but an organizer, coordinator, and facilitator. The large-group leader's responsibilities include—

- providing administrative leadership for the group;
- scheduling the study;
- promoting the study and coordinating enrollment efforts;
- enlisting and coordinating the work of small-group facilitators;
- ordering and distributing resources;
- maintaining and submitting accurate records of participation each week as Discipleship Training attendance;
- leading the large-group segments of the weekly group sessions.

The large-group leader should be someone who is interested in exploring the crucial truths of this course and who desires to help others grow in intimacy with God. A long list of qualifications and years of teaching experience are not required. A heart prepared by God— being available and teachable—is more important. Paramount to this leader's success is a strong commitment to study of this course and a faithful fulfillment of the basic responsibilities of group leadership.

This leader guide provides the large-group leader administrative help for organizing a Bible study group. It also gives specific guidance to prepare for and lead 11 group sessions.

Small-group facilitators. Enlist a small-group facilitator for every 10 to 12 participants. Again, these are not teachers but facilitators of the small groups' discussion and fellowship. Their responsibilities include—

- greeting and registering participants at the introductory session;

- calling members assigned to their small groups after the introductory session to introduce themselves, to tell them the locations of their small-group meeting rooms, and to encourage them to complete the daily assignments in week 1 of the member book;
- checking small-group members' attendance and homework prior to each week's meeting;
- taking prayer requests, conducting a prayer time at the beginning of the small-group period, praying for participants, and encouraging participants to pray for one another;
- guiding members to discuss the principal questions (listed at the beginning of each week's material in the member book) and the personal discussion questions (designated by colored type in the member book);
- promoting fellowship among group members;
- noting opportunities for follow-up ministry.

If you have 12 or fewer participants, one leader can serve both the large and small-group function. Each session of this guide designates the point during the session when small-group discussion is to occur. Share with each small-group facilitator a list of responsibilities and the following information about facilitating and handling problems in small groups.

FACILITATING SMALL-GROUP DISCUSSION

You will find many applications in this study for a contemporary walk with God. Beth Moore applies many of the course's concepts in her video presentations. In addition, the member book encourages participants to apply what they are learning as they complete their daily assignments.

One purpose of the small-group discussion period each week is to enable members to make meaningful application to their daily lives. Small-group facilitators will guide discussions of each week's principal questions, listed at the beginning of each week's material in the member book, as well as the personal discussion questions appearing in color in each day's lesson. Small-group facilitators can use the following guidelines to make these discussion times effective in challenging participants spiritually and promoting life change.

- Arrange the chairs in the meeting room in a circle or a semicircle so that participants can see one another. Seating should not physically exclude anyone.
- Greet members as they arrive and start the meeting on time. Allow 5 minutes for participants to share prayer requests; then pray or ask a participant to

pray. Make notes when prayer requests are shared. Assure members that you are concerned not only about their spiritual growth but also about their personal lives. Encourage them to pray for one another during the week. If someone is experiencing difficult circumstances, write a note or call between sessions to say that you are praying for them and that you care.

- Spend 20 minutes discussing the week's principal questions (listed at the beginning of the week's material in the member book) and 20 minutes discussing personal discussion questions (appearing in color in the member book). Emphasize that only participants who wish to respond should do so; no one is required to share responses. Do not force the discussion questions on members. Adapt and change them as necessary. Be flexible if members wish to spend more time on one group of questions or if they raise specific issues. Be sensitive to members' particular needs as the discussion progresses. Remember that your job is not to teach the material but to encourage and lead participants in sharing their insights about the work they have done during the week and in applying the content to their spiritual journeys.
- Be personally involved without relinquishing leadership. Your role as facilitator is that of a fellow disciple—one who shares the same struggles the other participants have in their spiritual lives. You need to be emotionally vulnerable and willing to share some of your own feelings and responses. However, you must also recognize that someone must lead the group and direct the discussion at all times. Be flexible but do not allow the discussion to veer off on a tangent. Keep the focus on the week's content and its application.
- Try to create a relaxed atmosphere that will help every member feel a sense of belonging. Use first names. Do not rush the discussion.
- Pray for the Holy Spirit's leadership; then allow Him freedom to direct the session as He wills. His movement may be evident in tears of joy or conviction, emotional or spiritual brokenness, or the thrill of a newfound insight. Be sensitive to signs of God's work in a person's life and follow up by asking the person to share. Giving participants the opportunity to testify to what God is doing is very important. Often, the testimony may help another person with a similar issue. Follow the Holy Spirit's leadership as God works in these discussion times.

- Be sure that you do not talk too much as facilitator. Do not be afraid of periods of silence.
- Be an encourager. Show a caring, loving spirit. Communicate acceptance and concern. Especially if your group includes non-Christians, you need to create an atmosphere that communicates, "I accept you as you are." Accepting participants does not necessarily mean that you agree with their values or choices. You can love a person without agreeing with that person. If a participant shares something that makes her feel vulnerable or ashamed, say something like: "I know your sharing took a lot of courage. I admire you for being willing to share it."
- Listen intently and aggressively. When someone shares something personal or painful, lean toward her. Use facial expressions to show concern. Nod your head.
- Be ready to address special needs that members may reveal. If someone is unsaved, follow the Holy Spirit's leadership to know the right time to talk with the person privately to lead her to Christ. If a participant reveals emotional pain or family problems, assure her of the group's concern and support and pause briefly to pray with the person. Then offer to meet with her later to help her find additional help if needed.
- Set boundaries. Do not permit a group member to act in a verbally abusive way toward another member. Do not force group members to do or say anything they are not willing to do or say. Try gently nudging a group member to a point of discovery and growth instead of pushing her to a conclusion for which she is not ready.
- Be enthusiastic!
- End the discussion period on time. You will face a challenge each week in bringing the discussion to an end in time for members to have a five-minute break before the large group reconvenes. At the first session emphasize the need to conclude on time each week. A few minutes before the time to end the discussion period, help the person speaking reach a point of closure. Then ask if anyone else has anything to add. Take time to respond, but at some point cut off the discussion. If someone is not finished, affirm the importance of what the person is saying. Offer to continue the discussion next week and ask that member to introduce the topic at the beginning of the next meeting. Or you may need to spend time privately with the person if the topic does not relate to the entire group. Be sure

you have tied loose ends. Did you put someone on hold during the discussion? Did you get back to the person? Was someone's sharing interrupted as you moved to focus on someone else's response? Did you reach closure with the original speaker? Finally, remind group members to pray for one another during the week.

COPING WITH PROBLEMS IN THE SMALL GROUP

No matter how meaningful the study and how effective the leadership, difficulties can arise in any group. Following are common problems and suggestions for dealing with them.

Absenteeism. Absentees miss a potentially life-changing experience and diminish others' learning. If a participant is absent, contact the person, communicate your concern, and encourage her to make up the work. Otherwise, a participant will quickly get further behind and likely drop out.

Not completing at-home assignments. Emphasize in the introductory session that a significant course requirement is doing daily study at home, including completion of the learning activities. State that each person's book will be checked before each session to see that homework was completed. Anyone who is not willing to make this commitment should not participate in the study.

If someone has not completed the week's assignments, encourage the person to stay up-to-date to gain the greatest benefits from the study. If someone continually refuses to complete the assignments, meet with her and suggest that she withdraw and participate at a time when she can devote herself adequately to the study.

Disagreement with the content. Some debate in a group is productive. Remember that the Scriptures should always be the final source of authority. If debate becomes counterproductive, suggest that you and the participant discuss the matter later so other members can participate in the present discussion.

Do not feel threatened if someone expects you to be an authority and to answer all of her questions. Emphasize your role as the facilitator of the discussion, pointing out that participants are to learn from one another and that you are not an authority on the subject. Suggest that a volunteer research the question during the week and report at the next meeting if the person insists that an answer is important to her.

A participant who dominates the group. Ways a person may dominate a group are—

- claiming a major portion of each discussion period to talk about her issues;
- repeatedly waiting until the last 10 minutes of a meeting to introduce an emotionally charged story or problem;
- attempting to block other group members' sharing;
- judging others' behavior or confessions;
- challenging your leadership in a hostile way;
- criticizing other group members' motives or feelings.

As the facilitator, make sure every person has an opportunity to share. Discourage dominating members by calling on others, by asking someone to speak who has not yet responded, or by focusing directly on someone else. If these methods do not work, talk privately with the dominating person and enlist the person's support in involving everyone in future discussions.

When a person is going into too much detail and is losing the attention of the group, you will usually notice that the group has disconnected. Direct the sharing back on course by discreetly interrupting the person and by restating the point she is trying to make: "So what you are saying is ...." Another method is to interrupt and restate the question you asked originally: "And Liz, what did you learn about God's love through that experience?" Even if the speaker is somewhat unsettled by this response, she should respond by restating the response more succinctly.

A SPECIAL CONCERN FOR *BREAKING FREE* GROUPS

Because of the nature of this study, leaders need to be aware of a potential problem in groups. Many people need to break free from behaviors that have their roots in childhood traumas or painful experiences. Thus, some group members may feel a need to talk about the details of their painful experiences. Such discussion can very well damage or destroy the group. Survivors of trauma do need to talk about their pain, but such emotional processing is not the purpose of this Bible study.

I have prepared a personal letter to each group member (pp. 30-31). Please duplicate the letter and go over it at the introductory session. If necessary review it again later in the study as appropriate. The letter validates the feelings of hurting members while helping them refrain from attempts to turn the group into a therapy session.

To you, the leader, I need to urge the same caution. The idea that you can help someone is very seductive. You may feel great pressure to direct the group into "helping" a hurting member. Please do not give in to the urge. Keep the focus of the group on truth and application of that truth. If the person needs counseling or a support group, help her find the assistance she needs. Avoid the mistake of allowing the group to lose its focus.

PLANNING STEPS

The following steps are suggested to assist the large-group leader in organizing a study of *Breaking Free*.

1. Enlist the support of your pastor. His endorsement will encourage people to deepen their spiritual lives. Perhaps he will agree to announce from the pulpit this discipleship opportunity.

2. Talk with the likely participants to determine the level of interest in this type of in-depth study. Also ask whether the study should be offered during the day, in the evening, or both. When scheduling the study, be sensitive to the needs of women who work outside the home.

3. Schedule 11 weeks on the church calender that will allow the greatest participation. Fall and spring studies usually result in more participation than summer sessions do. However, summertime may afford some persons with seasonal careers—such as schoolteachers—an opportunity to attend an intimate discipleship study.

4. Offer child care if possible. This will increase your attendance and ensure greater weekly participation.

5. If possible allow two hours for each weekly session. This time period will allow ample opportunities for both weekly activities: small-group discussion of the participants' home study and large-group viewing of the week's video presentation.

6. After estimating the number of participants, order member books (*Breaking Free*, item 0-7673-9112-8) between four and six weeks in advance by writing to the Customer Service Center; 127 Ninth Ave., North; Nashville, TN 37234; by calling toll free 1-800-458-2772; by sending a fax to 1 (615) 251-5933; by email at customer service@lifeway.com or by visiting a LifeWay Christian Store. Decide whether the church will pay for member books or whether participants will pay for their own. Experience has shown that if members pay for their books or a portion of the cost, they are likely to make a more serious commitment to the study. Make sure that scholarships are provided for members who cannot afford to purchase their own books.

7. Find a meeting room that will accommodate your large-group sessions and reserve it for the duration of the study. Also reserve small-group meeting rooms for the number of groups you will have. Arrange the meeting rooms to be as intimate as possible. Chairs in the small-group rooms should be arranged in circles or semicircles. Semicircular rows of chairs are acceptable for the large-group room as long as all participants can view the video.

8. Conduct a planning session for the large-group leader and the small-group facilitators. Complete the following actions in the meeting.

   - Obtain copies of this leader guide for your small-group facilitators. Discuss the group-session format and their responsibilities, which include:
     —greeting and registering participants at the introductory session;
     —calling members assigned to their small groups after the introductory session to introduce themselves, explain the locations of their small-group meeting rooms, and encourage them to complete the daily assignments for week 1;
     —checking small-group members' attendance and homework prior to each week's meeting;
     —taking prayer requests, conducting a prayer time at the beginning of the small-group period, praying for participants, and encouraging participants to pray for one another;
     —guiding members to discuss the principal questions (listed at the beginning of each week's material in the member book) and the personal discussion questions;
     —promoting fellowship among group members;
     —noting opportunities for follow-up ministry.
   - View the administrative segment on tape 1 of the video series provided in the leader kit.
   - Discuss registration procedures. Plan to set up several registration tables outside the large-group meeting room with signs indicating divisions of the alphabet. For example, participants whose last names begin with A–E will register at one station, F–J at the next, K–O at the next, P–S at the next, and T–Z at the final station. Assign small-group facilitators to handle registration at the stations. The members registered by a particular facilitator would become members of her group. Make adjustments if numbers fall unevenly. Instruct the facilitators to be at their stations 30 minutes before registration begins at the introductory session. Provide them with a supply of member books, registration cards, pencils, and reusable name tags. Tell each registrar that she has the responsibility of making a good first impression. She needs to wear a name tag, greet members with enthusiasm, answer their questions as best she can or promise to find out the answers, make them feel welcome, and direct them to the large-group session. At subsequent sessions the small-group facilitators will follow the same procedures to check attendance and homework.

- Explain that after the introductory session small-group facilitators will transfer names from their registration cards to attendance sheets that you will provide. Each week they will record attendance, completion of homework, and prayer requests on this sheet. Emphasize that facilitators are merely to check whether participants have responded to the learning activities in the member book, not to determine whether responses are correct.

9. Promote the study, using the suggestions in the following section.

10. Plan to keep accurate records and report attendance to the church office. Regardless of when the study is offered, it is a Discipleship Training study and should be reported as Discipleship Training participation on the Annual Church Profile. Another reason to keep accurate participation records is that participants can earn Christian Growth Study Plan diplomas for completing the study. For details see the requirements on page 223 of the member book.

11. Pray, pray, and keep praying that God will involve the members He desires and that He will validate this study with His obvious presence and activity!

PROMOTING THE STUDY

This study provides a wonderful opportunity for outreach because it is free of rules and does not require a particular church affiliation. Target persons in your community who are interested in Bible study. Church bulletins, newsletters, handouts, posters, fliers at Mothers' Day Out, announcements in worship services and in Sunday School classes, phone calls, and word of mouth are excellent and inexpensive ways to promote the study. Sometimes local radio and television stations announce upcoming events free of charge.

To assist you in promoting the study, we have provided two special promotional segments on tape 1 of the videos included in the leader kit. You may want to preview them now. You will find them immediately after the administrative segment and immediately before the introductory session. The first segment has been designed for your use inside the church—in a worship service, in a women's Bible study class, and in other locations where women regularly gather during the week. You have permission to duplicate this segment if you wish to create a loop tape that plays continually. Be sure to have someone prepared to announce the date, time, and place of the introductory session and to invite persons to attend. If the tape is left to play unattended, place a sign beside the monitor that lists the date, time, and place of the introductory session.

The second promotional segment is a 30-second commercial that can be used on a local television station or cable channel. We have left a blank screen for the last few seconds so that you can have the television station or cable company insert your personal invitation on the screen. Again, you have permission to duplicate this commercial as needed. If you would like a broadcast-quality copy of either the longer promotional segment or the television commercial, you may order one for the cost of the tape, plus labor, by calling Lee Sizemore at (615) 251-2882. Allow between two and three weeks for duplication and delivery.

Introductory Session

GOALS FOR THIS SESSION

In this session you will—
- register all members for *Breaking Free;*
- develop a role or attendance sheet;
- distribute member books and personal letter;
- welcome all members in joint session;
- explain basics about the format in joint session;
- view introductory video presentation.

BEFORE THE SESSION

1. If you are expecting 20 or more participants, set up tables in the designated meeting room with cards indicating a division of the alphabet at several stations. For example, those with last names beginning with letters A–E will sign up at one station, F–J at the next, and so forth.
2. Make copies of *personal letter* (pp. 30-31).
3. Enlist a volunteer or group leader to sit at each station. One way of distributing members to groups is to designate those each leader registers as members of her group. Adjustments will need to be made where numbers fall unevenly.
4. Each "registrar," whether leader or volunteer, should be at her station 30 minutes before registration is to begin. Each should be equipped with member books, registration cards or sign-up sheets (drawn up by your church or study leader), pens, and name tags.
5. Each registrar assumes the responsibility for the first impression of each new member. She needs to wear her name tag, be ready to greet new members with enthusiasm, anticipate questions with knowledgeable answers, make them feel welcome, and tell them what to do next. (After registration, members will report to joint session for the introductory session only. After this first introductory meeting, members will begin each week in their large groups for welcome, worship, and prayer.)

DURING THE SESSION

Introduction to *Breaking Free* (60 mins.)

1. Open introductory session in prayer.
2. Welcome members and introduce leaders. If your group is small, you might have each member introduce herself. You may want to create your own icebreaker to help introduce members to one another.

3. After introductions, the leader should give instructions and information concerning the course. This information will include the following and any additional points pertinent to your church facility:
A. Have members scan the first week's daily assignments. Make sure they understand that a week of study is to be completed prior to each weekly meeting. Before the next meeting, complete week 1. Make sure they understand that, although the daily assignments are crucial, members are urged to attend the weekly sessions even if their work is incomplete. Tell them to expect each daily assignment to take approximately 30–45 minutes.
B. Go over the *personal letter,* making clear the intent of the study. Stress the importance of seeking counseling or other support groups if a member feels the need. Express with great tenderness that there is no shame in needing to talk with someone, but we are concerned that they receive the wisest of counsel.
C. Encourage members to read the introduction in the member book and the *personal letter* from Beth before beginning their study.
D. Using the introduction to the member book, explain that the format and distinctive features of the book were designed to enhance learning. Point out that the Principal Questions, listed in the introduction to each unit, and the Personal Discussion Questions, appearing in color, will be discussed in the weekly group sessions.
E. Emphasize the primary reasons for small-group discussion are:
- to practice accountability—in-depth Bible studies are most often completed successfully in a group.
- to underscore the basic biblical truths that have been disclosed the previous week. This will be accomplished through discussing answers to the Principal Questions, which insure that the biblical information offered in the study has been received and understood.
- to see ways in which this study can be personally applied. This will be accomplished through discussing answers to the Personal Discussion Questions.

F. Express the extreme need to be good stewards of the time given for each session. The way time is organized can mean the success or failure of any group. Ask them to adopt the following time guidelines for the remaining sessions.
- Leaders: Be early!
- Members: Be on time!
- Small groups: Start on time! Leaders must make a habit from the beginning to start on time regardless of the number present.
- Members: Your personal comments are vital to the discussion time, but please make them brief and to the point in order to make the class run smoothly.

4. After today's introductory meeting, members will participate in a small group each week as well as a large group. (Tell them they will receive a phone call within 24 hours identifying their leader and telling them where their group will meet for discussion of sessions 1—10). Allow 45 minutes for small-group discussion divided according to the following schedule.
- Prayer requests and prayer (5 mins.). If you ask for prayer requests, ask that they be stated in one brief sentence. Be prepared to graciously intervene if a request becomes lengthy.
- Discussion of the Principal Questions and Personal Discussion Questions (40 mins.). Allow 7–8 minutes to discuss each day's assignment. Each day's Principal Questions can be answered in 2–3 minutes leaving 5–6 minutes for Personal Discussion Questions. Write these time divisions on a chalkboard for all members to keep in mind and be dedicated to enforcing them.

Introductory Video Presentation (50 mins.)

After group discussion, gather members in joint session to view the video which enhances and concludes each unit. Take 5 minutes for the transition. The video presentation will be 45–50 minutes.

Closing Remarks and Prayer (5 mins.)

1. After viewing the video, share any closing comments. Give a brief introduction to the next unit. This introduction may be as simple as saying, "This week our study is entitled, Untying the Cords of the Yoke."
2. Answer any questions, or if you do not know the answer, call the questioner as soon as you have the information she desires. Don't forget to take up name tags as the group departs.

AFTER THE SESSION

1. Compile all registration cards or lists and, if there are more than 12 members and more than 1 leader, divide the list of members into small groups. These discussion groups ideally need to be a maximum of 12 members.
2. Have leader(s) call members within the next 24 hours to introduce themselves and tell them where their group will meet the following week.
3. Have a leader or volunteer create attendance sheets from the registration cards so that every leader will be able to take roll of her individual group at each of the next 10 sessions. These attendance sheets need to be given to each leader prior to the next session.

I know you can do it. If you follow these guidelines you will have no problem being good stewards of the time period. As a leader, you can help insure learners are receiving the utmost from this study by implementing the suggestions you've received through this introduction.

God's Word changes lives! If a woman dedicates herself to the hours in God's Word this study will require, her life is undoubtedly going to be transformed. As a leader, be careful not to let your administration of this study eclipse your participation. Open God's Word and enjoy! Walk in faith toward making liberty in Christ a reality in life!

SESSION 1
Untying the Cords of the Yoke

BEFORE THE SESSION

1. Complete all of week 1 in the member book.
2. Pause and pray for each member of your group by name. Pray specifically that each will be teachable and that God will reveal Himself through this Bible study.
3. Pray for God's guidance in your preparation for this week's group session.
4. Carefully read through "During the Session" and make sure you are prepared for each question and activity that will take place at this week's group session.
5. Arrange your room to meet the needs of your group. An intimate setting seems to be most beneficial. If you have a group of 12 or under, arrange the chairs in a tight circle. If you have more than 12, 2 tight semicircles will work well.
6. If you are using the video, do the following:
   • Make sure all arrangements have been made to secure and set up necessary equipment.
   • If you have more than one small group, the arrangements need to be made in one room for the joint session. If you have only one group, the arrangements will be made in the room where the discussion group meets.
   • Preview the video and fill in your viewing guide. This step will be beneficial to you in case you are detained or distracted with administrative duties as the members watch the video.
   • Prepare several sentences, based on your response to the video, from which you can make closing remarks at the end of class just prior to dismissal.

Child Care Open, Attendance and Homework Check (15 mins.)

DURING THE SESSION
Large Group—Welcome, Worship, and Prayer (15 mins.)

1. Greet each member as she arrives and give her the name tag she used in the introductory session. Learn to call every participant by name.
2. Lead a time of worship and praise.
3. Pray, asking for God's presence and blessing throughout the session.
4. Dismiss to small groups.

Small Groups (45 mins.)

1. Ask for prayer requests and have prayer (5 mins.).
2. Review the Week's Principal Questions and Personal Discussion Questions (40 mins.).

Look for brief and basic answers to the principal questions just so you can be satisfied that the material was received and understood. Two to three minutes should be sufficient. All answers should be obvious as the reading and the learning activities of week 1 are performed and completed; however, make sure that you have written basic answers to the questions so that you can supply the information if a member does not volunteer or understand the answer.

Each day's Principal Question will be followed by a Personal Discussion Question. Personal Discussion Questions are identified in each day's study by appearing in color. The Personal Discussion Questions can be answered by anyone who feels comfortable sharing. Group members should feel no pressure to share their personal answers but should be given the opportunity if they wish. Please ask them always to be discreet and never to name another person who could be hurt by the discussion. Appropriate discussion of these questions will be invaluable to the application of the session. Leader, you must be ready and willing to redirect discussion if at any point it becomes inappropriate. Please pray for discretion and boldness on your part.

Day 1:
• *Principal Question:* Why do you think Uzziah would have been a hero to a boy like Isaiah?
• *Personal Discussion:* Based on all we've learned by Uzziah's example today, why do you think God hates pride as Proverbs 8:13 so vehemently states?

Day 2:
• *Principal Question:* How was Jotham similar to his father, and how was he different?
• *Personal Discussion:* Can you think of a time in your life when you allowed God to change your focus from someone else to Him? What were the circumstances?

Day 3:
- *Principal Question:* Why were high places accessible to a young and impressionable Ahaz?
- *Personal Discussion:* We might say that Manasseh "hit rock bottom" in verse 11. How might this terrible descent have been considered a "blessing in disguise"?

Day 4:
- *Principal Question:* Why do you think Hezekiah turned out so differently from his father?
- *Personal Discussion:* How do we also tend to flaunt our treasures to the godless, enjoying their favor and approval?

Day 5:
- *Principal Question:* How are we told Jesus returned to Galilee in Luke 4:14?
- *Personal Discussion:* Can you think of a few potential disasters from which Christ saved you since your initial experience of salvation?

If time allows, ask what ways God spoke directly to members in week 1.

Conclude 40-minute discussion time by thanking members for their willingness to share and affirming their apparent grasp of the material. If you are using the optional video, it is time to move into large group to view the video or turn on the video in the one small group. If you are not viewing the video, you may dismiss with a few introductory words about week 2 and a closing prayer at this time. Take the 5 remaining minutes in the first hour to prepare for the video.

Break and return to large group (5 mins.)

View the Video Presentation (50 mins.

Conclude Session (5 mins.)
- Leader gives a brief response to the video in one or two sentences.
- Leader gives a brief introduction to week 2 in her own words and encourages them to complete the next week's study before the next session.
- Leader closes with prayer. This would not be the time to take prayer requests. That opportunity was given at the beginning of the small-group session.
- Leader takes up name tags as group departs.

If you were able to abide by your time schedule, you will be able to dismiss on time. However, satisfy any unexpected but brief needs or comments that arise.

AFTER THE SESSION
1. Immediately record any concerns or impressions you had to pray for any member in your group while it is still fresh on your mind. Remember to pray for these throughout the week.
2. Evaluate session 1 by asking yourself the following questions and recording your answers:
   - Was I adequately prepared for today's session?
   - Was I able to begin and end session 1 on time?
   - If not, how can I help to make sure our time is used more wisely in session 2?
   - Do any members need extra encouragement this week? Note whether a card or a phone call would be appropriate; then, remember to follow up on each one.
   - What was my overall impression of session 1?
3. Read through "Before the Session" on page 12 so that you will know what preparations you'll need to make before your next session.
4. Have lunch with a friend, stop for a soft drink, have a cup of hot chocolate, or make time for a nap. Treat yourself to a moment's recreation for the work you've allowed God to accomplish through you!

JUST BETWEEN US

You and your group will need extra encouragement as you join me in memorizing Scripture. Pray, asking God to give you innovative ways to help your group learn and retain the Scriptures. You will surely reap the benefits as you continually hide His Word in your heart.

S E S S I O N 2
That You May Know

BEFORE THE SESSION

Refer to page 12 for a description of session procedures

Child Care Open, Attendance and Homework Check (15 mins.)

DURING THE SESSION

Large Group—Welcome, Worship, and Prayer (15 mins.)

1. Greet each member as she arrives and give her the name tag she used in the introductory session. Learn to call every participant by name.
2. Lead a time of worship and praise.
3. Pray, asking for God's presence and blessing throughout the session.
4. Dismiss to small groups.

Small Groups (45 mins.)

1. Ask for prayer requests and have prayer (5 mins.).
2. Review the Week's Principal Questions and Personal Discussion Questions (40 mins.).

Remember, Leader, you are looking for brief and basic answers to the Principal Questions that will indicate the comprehension of the reading and learning activities in week 2. Again, make sure that you are prepared to offer the answer in the event that a member does not volunteer. Also, be prepared to keep personal discussion within appropriate bounds.

Day 1:
- *Principal Question*: According to Isaiah 43:10-13, how would you describe the One you have been chosen to know, believe, and understand to be God?
- *Personal Discussion*: If you chose close and personal, what characteristics about your relationship reflect a degree of familiarity? If not, what causes you to feel distant from Him?

Day 2:
- *Principal Question*: According to Isaiah 43:7, why did God create us?
- *Personal Discussion*: Based on what we've learned from our Scriptures and definitions, what do you think being *created* for God's glory means now?

Day 3:
- *Principal Question*: Why do you think the writer of Psalm 63 had such a hunger and thirst for God?
- *Personal Discussion*: Can you think of a time in your life when you knew you should be satisfied but you weren't? Describe how you felt.

Day 4:
- *Principal Question*: According to Isaiah 48:18, what would happen if we paid attention to God's commands?
- *Personal Discussion*: What are a few other ways you can give God the opportunity to keep a spring of fresh water welling up within you?

Day 5:
- *Principal Question*: In Psalm 16:11, what did David confidently expect from God?
- *Personal Discussion*: We obviously and fortunately cannot escape God's presence, but why do you think we experience times when we sense God's presence more clearly than others?

If time allows, ask what ways God spoke directly to members in week 2.

Conclude the 40-minute discussion time by affirming your members in their participation today and their apparent grasp of the material. If you are using the video, move into large group to view the video or turn on the video in the one small group. If you are not viewing the video, you may dismiss with a few introductory words about week 3 and a closing prayer.

Break and return to large group (5 mins.)

View the Video Presentation (50 mins.)

Conclude Session (5 mins.)
- Leader gives a brief response to the video in one or two sentences.
- Leader gives a brief introduction to week 3 in her own words and encourages them toward the completion of their home study.

- Leader closes with prayer. Again, prayer requests will not be necessary since they were taken at the beginning of discussion.
- Leader takes up name tags as group departs.

AFTER THE SESSION

1. Immediately record any concerns or impressions you had to pray for any member in your group while it is still fresh on your mind. Remember to pray for these throughout the week.
2. Evaluate session 2 by asking yourself the following questions. Be sure to record your answers.

- Was I adequately prepared for today's session?
- Was I able to begin and end session 2 on time? If not, how can I make sure our time is used more wisely in session 3?
- Are there any members who may need extra encouragement this week? Note whether a card or phone call would be appropriate; then, remember to follow up on each one.
- What was my overall impression of session 2?

3. Read through "Before the Session" on page 12 so that you will know what preparations you'll need to make before your next session.

JUST BETWEEN US

This lesson could be life changing for many in your group as they wrestle with the subject matter of unbelief. We will also be looking into each of our hearts to let God identify areas in which we have set up our personal "idols." It may seem that this week we are giving up a great deal, but in fact we are just emptying out our hearts and hands so that they can be filled with the things of Christ.

Notes

_____

_____

_____

_____

_____

_____

_____

_____

_____

_____

S E S S I O N   3
Removing the Obstacles

BEFORE THE SESSION
Refer to page 12 for a description of session procedures.

Child Care Open, Attendance and Homework Check (15 mins.)

DURING THE SESSION
Large Group—Welcome, Worship, and Prayer (15 mins.)
1. Greet each member as she arrives and give her the name tag she used in the introductory session. Learn to call every participant by name.
2. Lead a time of worship and praise.
3. Pray, asking for God's presence and blessing throughout the session.
4. Dismiss to small groups.

Small Groups (45 mins.)
1. Ask for prayer requests and have prayer (5 mins.).
2. Review the Week's Principal Questions and Personal Discussion Questions (40 mins.).

Day 1:
- *Principal Question:* What was the theme of the encounter in Matthew 9:27-29?
- *Personal Discussion:* What are some obstacles you've battled in previous efforts to live the liberated, abundant life in Christ?

Day 2:
- *Principal Question:* What then do you think would be the biggest obstacle to glorifying God?
- *Personal Discussion:* Can you think of several reasons why we would have to cast down pride to break free from any areas of captivity? Name as many reasons as you can.

Day 3:
- *Principal Question:* What signs of idolatry did Isaiah see in the people (Isa. 2:8)?
- *Personal Discussion:* In retrospect, can you think of a time in which God was trying to lead you to find fullness in Him, but you settled for something less? ❏ Yes ❏ No   If so, what happened?

Day 4:
- *Principal Question:* With what are we to keep our "feet fitted" (Eph. 6:15)?
- *Personal Discussion:* Can you see ways in which any of these blessings or manifestations of the Holy Spirit could replace anxiety with peace? Please be specific.

Day 5:
- *Principal Question:* What does legalism mean when used in a negative, religious context?
- *Personal Discussion:* How could a student of God's Word squeeze the enjoyment out of her Christian walk by replacing relationship with regulations?

If time allows, ask what ways God spoke directly to members in week 3.

Conclude 40-minute discussion time by affirming your members in their participation today and their apparent grasp of the material. If you are using the optional video, move into large group to view the video or turn on the video in the one small group. If you are not viewing the video, you may dismiss with a few introductory words about week 4 and a closing prayer.

Break and return to large group (5 mins.)

View the Video Presentation (50 mins.)

Conclude Session (5 mins.)
- Leader gives a brief response to the video in one or two sentences.
- Leader gives a brief introduction to week 4 in her own words and encourages them toward the completion of their home study.
- Leader closes with prayer. Again, since prayer requests were taken at the beginning of discussion, they would not be necessary at this time.
- Leader takes up name tags as group departs.

AFTER THE SESSION
1. Immediately record any concerns or impressions you had to pray for any member in your group while it is still fresh on your mind. Remember to pray for these throughout the week.

2. Evaluate session 3 by asking yourself the following questions and recording your answers:
   - Was I adequately prepared for today's session?
   - Was I able to begin and end session 3 on time?
   - If not, how can I help to make sure our time is used more wisely in session 4?
   - Are there any members who may need extra encouragement this week? Note whether a card or phone call would be appropriate; then, remember to follow up on each one.
   - What was my overall impression of session 3?

3. Read through "Before the Session" on page 12 so that you will know what preparations you'll need to make before your next session.

JUST BETWEEN US

Take some time this week to reach out to your group to search out any needs of their hearts. Our God wants to do a mighty work in each life. Don't let the enemy get a foothold and discourage anyone from breaking free of the yoke that enslaves!

Notes

_____

_____

_____

_____

_____

_____

_____

_____

_____

_____

_____

_____

_____

S E S S I O N   4
Rebuilding the Ancient Ruins

BEFORE THE SESSION
Refer to page 12 for a description of session procedures.

Child Care Open, Attendance and Homework Check (15 mins.)

DURING THE SESSION
Large Group—Welcome, Worship, and Prayer (15 mins.)
1. Greet each member as she arrives and give her the name tag she used in the introductory session. Learn to call every participant by name.
2. Lead a time of worship and praise.
3. Pray, asking for God's presence and blessing throughout the session.
4. Dismiss to small groups.

Small Groups (45 mins.)
1. Ask for prayer requests and have prayer (5 mins.).
2. Review the Week's Principal Questions and Personal Discussion Questions (40 mins.).

Day 1:
- *Principal Question:* What might be a right reason or attitude for looking back at family history?
- *Personal Discussion:* Briefly describe a possible scenario of generational bondage—perhaps one you've witnessed personally.

Day 2:
- *Principal Question:* What is the difference between ungodly and godly jealousy?
- *Personal Discussion:* In your opinion, how could the moral to Gilda Radner's story parallel what we've talked about concerning generational bondage and generational sin?

Day 3:
- *Principal Question:* What is Satan's role in every human going astray (Rev. 12:9)?
- *Personal Discussion:* What behavior might you see in your life that you disliked in your parents or grandparents?

Day 4:
- *Principal Question:* In Jeremiah 18, what was the people's reply to God's willingness to remold and remake them?
- *Personal Discussion:* Without dishonoring anyone, what further enlightenment on chains you need to break has the Holy Spirit given you?

Day 5:
- *Principal Question:* What is Satan's priority in the lives of people who are already Christians?
- *Personal Discussion:* In what ways are you allowing the next generation to see authenticity in your life?

If time allows, ask what ways God spoke directly to members in week 4.

Conclude 40-minute discussion time by affirming your members in their participation today and their apparent grasp of the material. If you are using the optional video, move into large group to view the video or turn on the video in the one small group. If you are not viewing the video, you may dismiss with a few introductory words about week 5 and a closing prayer.

Break and return to large group (5 mins.)

View the Video Presentation (50 mins.)

Conclude Session (5 mins.)
- Leader gives a brief response to the video in one or two sentences.
- Leader gives a brief introduction to week 5 in her own words and encourages them toward the completion of their home study.
- Leader closes with prayer. Again, since prayer requests were taken at the beginning of discussion, they would not be necessary at this time.
- Leader takes up name tags as group departs.

AFTER THE SESSION
1. Immediately record any concerns or impressions you had to pray for any member in your group while it is still fresh on your mind. Remember to pray for these throughout the week.
2. Evaluate session 4 by asking yourself the following questions and recording your answers:

- Was I adequately prepared for today's session?
- Was I able to begin and end session 4 on time?
- If not, how can I help to make sure our time is used more wisely in session 5?
- Do any members need extra encouragement this week? Note whether a card or phone call would be appropriate; then, remember to follow up on each one.
- What was my overall impression of session 4?

3. Read through "Before the Session" on page 12 so that you will know what preparations you'll need to make before your next session.

JUST BETWEEN US

This chapter is in so many ways the basis of our entire Bible study. The things that God taught me as He rebuilt the ancient ruins of my life were literally life changing. I pray that you will experience some life-changing construction this week yourself. I am also claiming victory for your group as they meet with the best Architect of all time!

Notes

_____

_____

_____

_____

_____

_____

_____

_____

_____

_____

_____

_____

_____

_____

S E S S I O N 5
Binding Up the Brokenhearted

BEFORE THE SESSION
Refer to page 12 for a description of session procedures.

Child Care Open, Attendance and Homework Check (15 mins.)

DURING THE SESSION
Large Group—Welcome, Worship, and Prayer (15 mins.)
1. Greet each member as she arrives and give her the name tag she used in the introductory session. Learn to call every participant by name.
2. Lead a time of worship and praise.
3. Pray, asking for God's presence and blessing throughout the session.
4. Dismiss to small groups.

Small Groups (45 mins.)
1. Ask for prayer requests and have prayer (5 mins.).
2. Review the Week's Principal Questions and Personal Discussion Questions (40 mins.).

Day 1:
- *Principal Question:* According to Isaiah 61:1, who did God send Jesus to "bind up"?
- *Personal Discussion:* Think of a time when you suffered through a season with a broken heart. Can you remember one particular moment when, you felt your heart break? Did you have any idea at the time that God cared so much that He aimed His Son straight toward your heart?

Day 2:
- *Principal Question:* Based on Christ's statement in Matthew 18:6, how do you think one person could cause another person to sin?
- *Personal Discussion:* How could the enemy benefit from tempting you to believe wrongly about Christ's attitude toward child victimization?

Day 3:
- *Principal Question:* According to Timothy 2:26, why does the devil try to trap people?
- *Personal Discussion:* How could childhood victimization eventually trap someone by enticing conduct that could ruin the person in question?

Day 4:
- *Principal Question:* Why do you think Christ only considered Judas a betrayer even though all the disciples deserted Him and fled?
- *Personal Discussion:* Whether or not you fell to the temptation, chances are good you were tempted to react destructively over the days, weeks, or even months to come. What are a few things you felt like doing whether or not you did?

Day 5:
- *Principal Question:* How could the loss of faith turn into a form of bondage?
- *Personal Discussion:* Has the enemy turned any of your losses into bondage? If so, how?

If time allows, ask what ways God spoke directly to members in week 5.

Conclude 40-minute discussion time by affirming your members in their participation today and their apparent grasp of the material. If you are using the optional video, move into large group to view the video or turn on the video in the one small group. If you are not viewing the video, you may dismiss with a few introductory words about week 6 and a closing prayer at this time.

Break and return to large group (5 mins.)

View the Video Presentation (50 mins.)

Conclude Session (5 mins.)
- Leader gives a brief response to the video in one or two sentences.
- Leader gives a brief introduction to week 6 in her own words and encourages them toward the completion of their home study.
- Leader closes with prayer. Again, since prayer requests were taken at the beginning of discussion, they would not be necessary at this time.
- Leader takes up name tags as group departs.

AFTER THE SESSION
1. Immediately record any concerns or impressions you had to pray for any member in your group while it is

still fresh on your mind. Remember to pray for these throughout the week.

2. Evaluate session 5 by asking yourself the following questions and recording your answers:
   - Was I adequately prepared for today's session?
   - Was I able to begin and end session 5 on time?
   - If not, how can I help to make sure our time is used more wisely in session 6?

- Are there any members who may need extra encouragement this week? Note whether a card or phone call would be appropriate; then, remember to follow up on each one.
- What was my overall impression of session 5?

3. Read through "Before the Session" on page 12 so that you will know what preparations you'll need to make before your next session.

JUST BETWEEN US

Oh, my beloved Friends, this week of study was written mostly by my precious Savior as He carried me in His arms. I have experienced several events that have broken my heart in one way or another over the last several years. I know firsthand Who is able to bind up every broken heart. I'll pray with you that your group is open to being ministered to by the great Physician.

Notes

_____

_____

_____

_____

_____

_____

_____

_____

_____

_____

_____

_____

SESSION 6

Beauty from Ashes

BEFORE THE SESSION

Refer to page 12 for a description of session procedures.

Child Care Open, Attendance and Homework Check (15 mins.)

DURING THE SESSION

Large Group—Welcome, Worship, and Prayer (15 mins.)

1. Greet each member as she arrives and give her the name tag she used in the introductory session. Learn to call every participant by name.
2. Lead a time of worship and praise.
3. Pray, asking for God's presence and blessing throughout the session.
4. Dismiss to small groups.

Small Groups (45 mins.)

1. Ask for prayer requests and have prayer (5 mins.).
2. Review the Week's Principal Questions and Personal Discussion Questions (40 mins.).

Day 1:
- *Principal Question:* In what ways did Tamar symbolize and express her grief?
- *Personal Discussion:* What is your personal opinion regarding the advice Absalom gave Tamar?

Day 2:
- *Principal Question:* What has the bride of Christ done according to Revelation 19:4-8?
- *Personal Discussion:* Think once again of the implications of the term *bride*. What are a few things the word *bride* implies that the word *wife* may not?

Day 3:
- *Principal Question:* According to Ephesians 5:32, what is far more profound than a man and woman coming together in marriage?
- *Personal Discussion:* Read Song of Songs 5:10-16. In the eyes of His beloved, which will be you, how will Christ look? Give your own descriptions based on these verses.

Day 4:
- *Principal Question:* How could a barren woman have more "children" than a married woman who actually gave birth?
- *Personal Discussion:* Have you ever received something you desperately wanted but still felt an unsatisfied longing you couldn't identify? ❑ Yes ❑ No If so, explain.

Day 5:
- *Principal Question:* What result did Christ guarantee if His followers put into practice what He demonstrated to them?
- *Personal Discussion:* How about you? Can you think of a time when you sensed the fullness and favor of God but would not characterize the time as happy? Explain.

If time allows, ask in what ways God spoke directly to members in week 6.

Conclude 40-minute discussion time by affirming your members in their participation today and their grasp of the material. If you are using the optional video, move into large group to view the video or turn on the video in the one small group. If you are not viewing the videotaped lecture, you may dismiss with a few introductory words about week 7 and a closing prayer.

Break and return to large group (5 mins.)

View the Video Presentation (50 mins.)

Conclude Session (5 mins.)
- Leader gives a brief response to the videotape in one or two sentences.
- Leader gives a brief introduction to week 7 in her own words and encourages them toward the completion of their home study.
- Leader closes with prayer. Again, since prayer requests were taken at the beginning of discussion, they are unnecessary at this time.
- Leader takes up name tags as group departs.

AFTER THE SESSION

1. Immediately record any concerns or impressions you had to pray for any member of your group while it is still fresh on your mind. Remember to pray for these throughout the week.

2. Evaluate session 6 by asking yourself the following questions and recording your answers:
   - Was I adequately prepared for today's session?
   - Was I able to begin and end session 6 on time?
   - If not, how can I help to make sure our time is used more wisely in session 7?
   - Do any members need extra encouragement this week? Note whether a card or phone call would be appropriate; then, remember to follow up on each one.
   - What was my overall impression of session 6?

3. Read through "Before the Session" on page 12 so that you will know what preparations you'll need to make before your next session.

JUST BETWEEN US

Can you believe that we have six whole weeks behind us on our journey? It is my prayer that everyone in your group will walk into Bible study wearing her crown of beauty and leaving the ashes in the nail-scarred hands.

Notes

_____

_____

_____

_____

_____

_____

_____

_____

_____

_____

_____

_____

SESSION 7
The Potter and the Clay

BEFORE THE SESSION
Refer to page 12 for a description of session procedures.

Child Care Open, Attendance and Homework Check (15 mins.)

DURING THE SESSION
Large Group—Welcome, Worship, and Prayer (15 mins.)
1. Greet each member as she arrives and give her the name tag she used in the introductory session. Learn to call every participant by name.
2. Lead a time of worship and praise.
3. Pray, asking for God's presence and blessing throughout the session.
4. Dismiss to small groups.

Small Groups (45 mins.)
1. Ask for prayer requests and have prayer (5 mins.).
2. Review the Week's Principal Questions and Personal Discussion Questions (40 mins.).

Day 1:
- *Principal Question:* How did God's children cheat themselves through rebellion (Isa. 30:8-21)?
- *Personal Discussion:* Can you recall a situation in which you acted pigheaded toward God?

Day 2:
- *Principal Question:* What happens if we continue in rebellion, rejecting God's Word, relying on oppression, and depending on deceit?
- *Personal Discussion:* Have you sometimes experienced defeat because you refused to calm yourself in the presence of God and trust Him?

Day 3:
- *Principal Question:* What is God's will according to John 6:39-40?
- *Personal Discussion:* Have you ever noticed that you can experience freedom in one part of your life while you are still in bondage in another? If so, describe a time when you were free in one area while bound in another.

Day 4:
- *Principal Question:* Because the Lord is so compassionate, what can He do with the ruins, deserts, and wastelands of His children's lives (Isa. 51:3)?
- *Personal Discussion:* Do you also have authority problems? If so, how have you become aware of them?

Day 5:
- *Principal Question:* Why would walking with God be so much wiser and personally fulfilling than asking God to walk with us?
- *Personal Discussion:* What is your biggest temptation when you don't feel that God is illuminating your way clearly?

If time allows, ask ways in which God spoke directly to members in week 7.

Conclude 40-minute discussion time by affirming your members in their participation today and their apparent grasp of the material. If you are using the optional video, move into large group to view the video or turn on the video in the one small group. If you are not viewing the video, you may dismiss with a few introductory words about week 8 and a closing prayer.

Break and return to large group (5 mins.)

View the Video Presentation (50 mins.)

Conclude Session (5 mins.)
- Leader gives a brief response to the video in one or two sentences.
- Leader gives a brief introduction to week 8 in her own words and encourages them toward the completion of their home study.
- Leader closes with prayer. Again, since prayer requests were taken at the beginning of discussion, they would not be necessary at this time.
- Leader takes up name tags as group departs.

AFTER THE SESSION
1. Immediately record any concerns or impressions you had to pray for any member of your group while it is still fresh on your mind. Remember to pray for these throughout the week.

2. Evaluate session 7 by asking yourself the following questions and recording your answers:
   • Was I adequately prepared for today's session?
   • Was I able to begin and end session 7 on time?
   • If not, how can I help make sure our time is used more wisely in session 8?
   • Do any members need extra encouragement this week? Note whether a card or phone call would be appropriate; then, remember to follow up.
   • What was my overall impression of session 7?

3. Read through "Before the Session" on page 12 so that you will know what preparations you'll need to make before your next session.

JUST BETWEEN US

Keith and I always have a good laugh over our girls as they try to figure out a way NOT to obey us and yet still appear obedient. There is no such thing as partial obedience when parenting or when following Christ. Is He the boss? Many of your members might have a struggle this week over the issue of authority. I pray that God will guide you as you guide them from His wonderful instruction book!

Notes

S E S S I O N   8
God's Unfailing Love

BEFORE THE SESSION

Refer to page 12 for a description of session procedures. Refer to page 24 and follow for beginning the small group. Procedure will be the same to the subhead "Small Groups." At this point come back to this page.

Small Groups (45 mins.)

1. Ask for prayer requests and have prayer (5 mins.).
2. Review the Week's Principal Questions and Personal Discussion Questions (40 mins.).

Day 1:

- *Principal Question*: What does Proverbs 20:6 suggest about unfailing love?
- *Personal Discussion*: How would you explain the difference between God's love and human love, even at its best? Offer several examples of how God's love differs.

Day 2:

- *Principal Question*: Why should the rebellious who have been freed be faithful to tell of His works?
- *Personal Discussion*: Why do you think we readily accept God's love for others but struggle with the belief that He loves us equally, radically, completely, and unfailingly? In the margin list as many reasons as you can.

Day 3:

- *Principal Question*: What happens when someone acknowledges that Jesus is the Son of God?
- *Personal Discussion*: Can you think of a time when you were suddenly awash with the magnitude of God's love for you personally? Describe it.

Day 4:

- *Principal Question*: Why could not believing God personally and lavishly loves us be a sin?
- *Personal Discussion*: List every way you know he/she loves you. Really give this activity some thought.

Day 5:

- *Principal Question*: Since we know God loves us unfailingly at all times, what do you think "abiding" or "remaining" in God's love means?

- *Personal Discussion*: Contrast two children: one who believes he or she is loved and the other who does not.

Please turn to page 24 and repeat the procedure given there to the following segment. Reminder: You will give a brief introduction to week 9 rather than week 8.

AFTER THE SESSION

1. Immediately record any concerns or impressions you had to pray for any member of your group while it is still fresh on your mind. Remember to pray for these throughout the week.
2. Evaluate session 8 by asking yourself the following questions and recording your answers:
   - Was I adequately prepared for today's session?
   - Was I able to begin and end session 8 on time?
   - If not, how can I help make sure our time is used more wisely in session 9?
   - Are there any members who may need extra encouragement this week? Note whether a card or phone call would be appropriate; then, remember to follow up on each one.
   - What was my overall impression of session 8?
3. Read through "Before the Session" on page 12 so that you will know what preparations you'll need to make before your next session.

JUST BETWEEN US

We have tackled so many tough issues during the course of this study. How wonderful it is to bask in His unfailing love. I hope you are feeling loved by Him. I hope you know how much I love each of you and your faithfulness to His Word.

SESSION 9

The Steadfast Mind

BEFORE THE SESSION

Refer to page 12 for a description of session procedures. Refer to page 24 and follow for beginning the small group. Procedure will be the same to the subhead "Small Groups." At this point come back to this page.

Refer to Before the Session and videotape for week 10 for the closing exercise. On the videotape I ask members to write a letter to God. You will need to do one of two things. Either plan for a get-together after the final session to complete the assignment, or you will need to make the letter assignment this week so it can be completed next week.

Small Groups (45 mins.)

1. Ask for prayer requests and have prayer (5 mins.).
2. Review the Week's Principal Questions and Personal Discussion Questions (40 mins.).

Day 1:

- *Principal Question:* What can happen to those who have *knowledge of God* but *don't think it worthwhile to retain it?*
- *Personal Discussion:* By any chance, are you still waiting to see the first signs of fruit from a previous valley? Can you think of ways God could use the lapse of time to bring forth an even greater harvest?

Day 2:

- *Principal Question:* How does God desire to lead His children?
- *Personal Discussion:* Think about a stronghold you've experienced. What part did insecurity play? Explain in general terms.

Day 3:

- *Principal Question:* What is the difference between casual thoughts and captivating thoughts?
- *Personal Discussion:* Why do you think we, like the ancient Israelites, tend to avoid dealing with the high places in our lives? What do you think could happen in our lives and possibly the next generation or two if we also neglect casting down the high places (strongholds)?

Day 4:

- *Principal Question:* What do you think the Old Testament means by the phrase *high places?*
- *Personal Discussion:* Describe a little about your own experience with a stronghold and note a few specific lies the enemy used. As always, be general if the subject concerns a sensitive issue or something private.

Day 5:

- *Principal Question:* What is God's goal for our thought lives?
- *Personal Discussion:* In your own words and from your best recollection, how did the character in the illustrations go from captive to captor?

Please turn to page 24 and repeat the procedure given there to the following segment. Reminder: You will give a brief introduction to week 10 rather than week 8.

AFTER THE SESSION

1. Immediately record any concerns or impressions you had to pray for any member of your group while it is still fresh on your mind. Remember to pray for these throughout the week.
2. Evaluate session 9 by asking yourself the following questions and recording your answers:
   - Was I adequately prepared for today's session?
   - Do any members need extra encouragement this week? Note whether a card or phone call would be appropriate; then, remember to follow up.
   - What was my overall impression of session 9?
3. Read through "Before the Session" on page 12 so that you will know what preparations you'll need to make before your final session.

JUST BETWEEN US

Beloved, can you believe just one week remains in our time together? What a journey this has been! This week we will see just how important our minds are. I pray that you will be able to communicate to your group how imperative it is to surrender up their minds to the control of our Savior.

SESSION 10
The Display of His Splendor

BEFORE THE SESSION

Refer to page 12 for a description of session procedures.

Prepare for the closure exercise. Watch the videotape. If you made the assignment with session 9, you may have the envelope-sealing activity with this session. Otherwise, if possible, have a final celebration meeting. Seal the envelopes as per instructions on the videotape.

Child Care Open, Attendance and Homework Check (15 mins.)

DURING THE SESSION

Large Group—Welcome, Worship, and Prayer (15 mins.)

1. Greet each member as she arrives and give her the name tag she used in the introductory session. Learn to call every participant by name.
2. Lead a time of worship and praise.
3. Pray, asking for God's presence and blessing throughout the session.
4. Dismiss to small groups.

Small Groups (45 mins.)

1. Ask for prayer requests and have prayer (5 mins.).
2. Review the Week's Principal Questions and Personal Discussion Questions (40 mins.).

Day 1:
- *Principal Question:* What is God's absolute priority commandment for you and me?
- *Personal Discussion:* Read each of the references below and write any insight you gain concerning our representation as an oak, a strong tree planted by the Lord: Psalm 1:1-4; Isaiah 60:21; Jeremiah 17:7-8; Matthew 12:33.

Day 2:
- *Principal Question:* What is the desire of the hearts of those "walking in the way" of His laws?
- *Personal Discussion:* Think of someone who helped authenticate some part of God's Word as a witness to you. What about his/her life made you think, "It is true"?

Day 3:
- *Principal Question:* What did God promise in His covenant with Israel in Genesis 15:14?
- *Personal Discussion:* Please use the space below and name your plunder. Don't feel uncomfortable. You are boasting in the Lord your God! By His mighty power, you have escaped richer than before.

Day 4:
- *Principal Question:* According to Isaiah 58:6, what kind of fast has God chosen?
- *Personal Discussion:* Think of the last time obedience to God was momentarily not much fun. Describe the experience in general terms.

Day 5:
- *Principal Question:* According to Isaiah 40:28-31, whose strength will the Lord renew?
- *Personal Question:* Can you confirm experientially the concept we're considering? Offer a little feedback in the space below concerning the relationship between weariness and self-effort or renewed strength and the presence of God.

If time allows, ask what ways God spoke directly to members in week 10.

Conclude the 40-minute discussion time by affirming their participation throughout the last 10 weeks and their grasp of material that was often difficult. If you are using the optional video, move into large group to view the last segment or turn on the video in the one small group. If you are not using the video, you may dismiss with concluding remarks and a closing prayer at this time.

Break and return to large group (5 mins.)

View the Video Presentation (50 mins.)

Conclude Session (10 mins. rather than 5, if you are doing an optional evaluation)
- If you prepared an evaluation, distribute it at this time and allow 5 minutes to complete it.
- Leader offers closing remarks to *Breaking Free*.
- Leader closes with prayer.
- Leader has a good laugh or a good cry depending on which seems appropriate!

AFTER THE SESSION

1. Evaluate session 10 by asking yourself the following concluding questions and recording your answers:
   - Did members seem to grasp the over all principals emphasized in this 10-week study?
   - Are there group members with no church home who I should invite to visit church with me?
   - Should I remain in contact with any members of my group for the purpose of encouragement?
   - Would I consider *taking* another course of this kind?
   - Would I consider *leading* another course of this kind?
   - What was my overall impression of *Breaking Free?*

2. Consider letting us hear from you. If God has spoken to you or done something significant in your life or the lives of one of your members as a direct result of this Bible study, we would love for you to share a brief testimony with us. Write to us, including your name, address, phone number, and church affiliation, and mail your testimony to:

Adult Discipleship and Family Department
Dale McCleskey, Editor, MSN 151
127 Ninth Avenue, North
Nashville, Tennessee 37234-0151

JUST BETWEEN US

As we come to this week of study, I wish I could see your faces in person! We have shared such a personal time and I thank you for joining me. If I could see you, I know your faces would be aglow with His glory. I know that your hearts and your hands would be emptied of all that had encumbered them from the past. I know that I could see Him reflected in your faces. Thank you for letting Him work in your life and for sharing your life with your group.

You are the best!

Notes

_____

_____

_____

_____

_____

_____

_____

_____

_____

A personal note to you from Beth

You may have traveled with me on previous Bible study journeys. I need to tell you about some important differences between those journeys and this one. Every one of the studies God has led me to write has a specific purpose. *A Woman's Heart* seeks to understand God's relationship to His children. *A Heart Like His* seeks to understand how we relate to God, and *To Live Is Christ* explores sold-out servanthood. In each of those studies we followed the lives of biblical characters to learn from them. We played the roles of students and observers. This time we play a more personal part. We are the character in this study. We are the beloved subject God wants to directly address in this study.

This difference in focus demands that I share the following information with you and that you seek to understand it thoroughly. Keep this note in your workbook. You may need to refer to it. Satan would love to cause confusion and destruction in your Breaking Free group. The message I am sharing with you now is critical to see that he does not succeed.

Christ builds the church on several different ministries. These different ministries have different tasks or functions.

- The teaching ministry exists to help people learn the truth of God's Word and how to apply it to life.
- The outreach ministry of the church exists to introduce people to Christ and bring them into His body, the church.
- The preaching ministry exists to proclaim Christ's truth.
- Worship ministry exists to praise God.

One organizational unit of the church may help to fulfill several of these ministries, but every organizational unit or group must have a focus—a purpose. For example, Sunday School typically exists to combine outreach, teaching God's word, and fellowship between believers. Discipleship exists to train believers in some specific way such as how to teach, how to be a better mate or parent, or how to study God's Word. Now comes my critical point: Every group within the body of Christ has a purpose. Much confusion and harm often results when someone either does not understand or chooses to ignore that purpose.

Imagine with me a common occurance in church life. A group comes together. In that group of 10 people, two want to do in-depth Bible study. Two want to do evangelism. Two need help with marital problems. One wants to fellowship. Three don't know what they want. See the problem? I have seen believers shred each other in various ways because they didn't clearly state and stick to their purpose. Much opportunity for Satan can be avoided by adopting a clear purpose for the group. Then everyone knows the identity and purpose. They can be comfortable because they know where the boundaries lie.

Because of the content of Breaking Free, we need to consider two specific kinds of groups: in-depth Bible studies and support groups. Both groups can be very important, even lifesaving, but please do not confuse the two.

Bible study builds the foundation. The focus of Bible study is truth. Breaking Free is a Bible study. Our purpose is to work together to understand and apply truth to our lives.

One of the distinctions of Bible study is universality. Everyone needs Bible study. Everyone needs a strong foundation. Bible study represents the teaching function of the church.

Support groups assist people to deal with and overcome specific issues in their lives. Some *people have a specialized need. They may have been abused as children. They need a safe environment to deal with past pain and buried emotions. They may have developed a powerful addiction that requires a high level of support and accountability.*

Support groups are specific rather than universal. Not everyone needs a support group. Support groups meet specific needs. Support groups represent the healing ministry of the church. Support groups particularly help members deal with grief. I believe they express the koinonia, family love, of Christ's body.

Bible studies and support groups serve different purposes. They require different covenants and different leadership. In the study of Breaking Free, some people will discover a need for additional work. They may discover past pain that calls for a time of grieving. They may discover deeply-rooted behaviors in need of change. For some, counseling may be best. For others, a support group may provide answers.

I want to affirm the validity of those needs and ask you to keep this group focused on Bible study. If the content of Breaking Free causes you to recognize a need to deal with an addiction or with some ungrieved loss, I encourage you to seek proper help.

Here is a plan for seeking help. No one answer will fit every person, so consider these possibilities. If you need to deal with pain growing from your childhood, present marital pain, or an out-of-control behavior.

> *1. Talk with your pastor or another church staff minister. He or she may be able to help you or refer you to qualified groups or counselors.*
>
> *2. Talk with a Christian counselor who is qualified in your specific area of need.*
>
> *3. Find a Christ-centered support group that can provide you the support you need. On page 92 of the member's book you will find suggested resources for Christ-centered support groups.*

Some issues in our lives are extremely painful. We need a listening ear; however, please do not make the mistake of seeking therapy from your Bible study group. Our purpose in Breaking Free is to explore truth. If you discover some deeper needs in your life, you may need to process those issues privately with a trained counselor or a support group. If you have a need to process deeper emotional issues, we will love and support you as you seek the additional help you need.

Allow me to share a significant Scripture with you. In 1 Corinthians 14 Paul was discussing order in the church. Some people felt compelled to share their message. Thus they were dominating and creating disorder. Paul wrote in verse 32, "The spirits of prophets are subject to the control of prophets." He was reminding them that they could contain themselves.

Paul's words apply to us in the same way. We may need to process griefs and regrets. Sometimes that need can seem overwhelming. Our needs are important, but we need to exercise good boundaries. We only ought to share the intimate details of our lives with an appropriate group or counselor.

Please don't allow these cautions to frighten you in any way. I just want to help you avoid an obstacle Satan would love to throw in the way of you and your group. I'm praying for you as you make liberty in Christ a greater reality in your life.

Your freed sister,

Beth Moore